MW01042506

Leading To Easter

Sermons And Worship Resources

CSS Publishing Company, Inc., Lima, Ohio

LEADING TO EASTER

Copyright © 2002 by
CSS Publishing Company, Inc.
Lima, Ohio

For more information about CSS Publishing Company resources, visit our website at www.csspub.com or e-mail us at custserv@csspub.com or call (800) 241-4056.

ISBN 0-7880-1931-7   PRINTED IN U.S.A.

Table Of Contents

A Season In Purgatory

A Service And
Sermon For Ash Wednesday

Stan Purdum

A Service Of Worship For
Ash Wednesday

Welcome and Announcements

Prelude

Call To Worship

Leader: The journey of Lent begins this day.

People: A road that leads to the Cross.

Leader: There are other roads we'd rather walk.

People: Other pathways more upbeat.

Leader: But this road takes us closer to God.

People: Then we must follow this path.

Leader: Now is the season for learning and giving.

People: Thank you, God, that you make the journey with us.

Leader: Thank you, God, that we travel not alone.

Hymn
"Lord, Who Throughout These Forty Days"

Opening Prayer
Lord of life, death, and beyond, please accept our worship and praise this evening. May this service be to us an opening of our minds, hearts, and spirits, that we might perceive your direction and receive your call that we may grow closer to you in this season. In the name of Jesus. Amen.

Prayer Response
"It's Me, O Lord, Standing In The Need Of Prayer"

Old Testament (*read responsively*)
Psalm 139:1-12, 23-24

Hymn
"When We Are Living"

Presenting Our Offerings
Offertory
Doxology

New Testament
Luke 18:9-14

Choir Anthem

Sermon
A Season In Purgatory
"God, be merciful to me, a sinner!" — Luke 18:13

Prayer
Lord God, we cannot escape that Lent is a time of introspection and confession, a time to look at what is unworthy of you in our lives and try to reform it or cast it out.

Our humanity is your gift to us, O God, so let us value it and not use it as an excuse to continue in our sins. But while our humanness is precious, it is not divinity, and so we may fail. Thus we ask for your help to become the people you want us to be. When we fall short, when we sin, when we falter, help us to rise again, to doggedly follow the footsteps of the Man of Galilee, the Christ of the Cross, the Exalted Lord of Easter.

Thank you for Jesus' steadfast obedience to your will, even unto death. In his name. Amen.

The Imposition Of Ashes
"Repent, and believe the Gospel."

Hymn
"Pass Me Not, O Gentle Savior"

Benediction

Postlude

A Season In Purgatory

Psalm 139:1-12, 23-24
Luke 18:9-14

When's the last time you had a speeding ticket? While nobody likes getting them, here in America, a lot of people think it's no big deal. A ticket might run you 75 or 100 bucks, but for most people, that's not too great a hardship. In fact, some people in jobs that take them on the road consider an occasional speeding ticket simply part of the cost of doing business.

Be glad you don't live in Finland. There, when you are fined for speeding, it's levied on a scale graded not only by how much over the limit you were going, but also according to your income. Thus an Internet entrepreneur speeding in his BMW recently was fined in Finnish marks the equivalent of $71,400. A corporate director, buzzing along at a similar speed, was fined $14,500. For someone who is poor, the fine can be as low as $63.

These fines are not applied according to how the traffic officer feels that day, but according to a precise formula. In Finland, everyone's net monthly income figure is available by computer, and the officer can get the figure right away by making a cell phone call. They take your monthly income, reduce it by 1,500 Finnish marks, and divide the total by 60. Then, for each dependent, they deduct another 15 marks. If you own real estate, they add 20 marks. This final figure, called a day fine, is then multiplied by a number from one to 120, depending on how severe your violation was.

Martin Marty, who described Finland's speeding-fine system in a magazine column, commented that this system would never go in America, where all the wealthy have good lawyers.

Marty went on to point out that Finland's system is akin to the old Catholic idea of purgatory. In Catholic thought, purgatory is a way station after death on the road to heaven, a place where the deceased are purged of any unforgiven minor sins before being admitted into their final reward. The idea behind purgatory was measurement: How long should someone stay? How hot will things get? How severe will be the punishment? People wanted to know these things so they could figure how much they'd have to endure before they finally got to the pearly gates.[1]

Protestant reformers rejected the doctrine of purgatory, pointing out that it is not mentioned in the Bible and asserting that salvation is obtained by faith in Christ alone, with no period of pre-heaven cleansing necessary.

We are Protestants and so, unlike our Catholic brethren, we have no theology of purgatory, but we find it a useful word nonetheless. In common parlance, "purgatory" has come to refer to hard times on this side of the grave, periods of trouble that in some sense we have brought on ourselves as a result of personal wrongdoing, inattention, or even plain old sloppiness.

A friend who works in publishing told me about a problem he fell into where the word "purgatory" fit. As a result of some failure to communicate with a freelance writer as clearly as he thought he had, he received from that writer material that was a mere rehash of a book the company had previously published. This was just four days before deadline. The company couldn't cancel the book because they had already advertised it and even had some orders for it. Thus, in a matter of four days, my friend and another editor rewrote the book. They barely slept and worked throughout the workdays and evenings of all four days. It was not fun. Purgatory seemed a fitting word as my friend paid for his "sin" of unclear communication.

But despite the temporary pain, my friend says, he derived a certain satisfaction from having the opportunity to fix the problem. That's the beauty of purgatory. You get to pay for what you messed up so that in the end you are even-Steven and appropriately tidied up for residency in glory.

Here's what troubles me more. If the everyday use of "purgatory" refers to self-induced problems that we get a chance to square up, what about problems or sins we commit for which there is nothing we can do to atone, no way to undo our mistakes or wrongdoings?

Let me give you an example from my own history: In my younger days, I managed a church camp. I oversaw the property, hired staff, and ran the camp programs. During the first spring I was there, I laid out several day hikes into a state park that was adjacent to the camp. In the park, there's a deep gorge, and I decided that one of our hikes should go down into it. There were a few trails down already, but when I got to the one that worked best for the route I was laying out, it was marked "Closed." Nonetheless, it was not blocked off, so I decided to walk down it myself and see if it was passable. It was. In fact, I had a backpack on my back. Even loaded like that, I found the trail, which switchbacked down the gorge, steep but not too difficult. So I set that as a hike for the campers.

That summer, I sent several groups of campers with their counselors on that route, and they all did okay until midsummer, when the counselor in one group heading down, a young woman in her early twenties, suddenly slipped and had a bad fall, breaking her knee. We had to have rescue workers haul her out of the gorge.

Later, when I saw her in the hospital, they were getting ready to operate on her knee, and I knew that no matter how it came out, her knee would never be as good as new.

The young woman herself was very gracious about it, and blamed nobody but herself, but I felt responsible nonetheless. I had decided that our campers could use a closed route, so it was because of my decision that she was on that path at all. Obviously, I meant no harm to come to her, but I felt bad anyway, and I still do, whenever I think of her. It would be nice to have some sort of emotional purgatory I could go through and then think of it no more, but that's not the way things are. There's no way I can go back and undo the decision I had made.

Here's one more example. At a church we once attended, the pastor, for his youth confirmation class, asked me to be a mentor for a twelve-year-old boy named Jeremy. The membership program this pastor was using involved each candidate meeting once a week with his or her mentor and the two working that week's lesson together. I agreed to be a mentor. Jeremy came from a broken home and lived with his mother, but once a week she delivered Jeremy to my residence and we worked through the membership lesson for the week. I found Jeremy was a quiet kid, but he

11

once showed me some cartoons he'd been drawing that involved a superhero he'd created. I noticed a pretty violent thread in the cartoons, but not knowing Jeremy well, I merely complimented him on his drawing talent.

Well, time went on, he and I completed the course, and Jeremy was eventually received into the church. Shortly after that, however, he and his mother relocated to another community, and they stopped attending our church. I lost track of Jeremy, but one day, about four years later, I ran into him at the mall, though I had to look twice to make sure it really was him. Naturally he had grown and changed physically, but more than that, he'd adopted a style of appearance that seemed designed to be in the face of society. He had spiky hair and was wearing leather pants, a fishnet T-shirt, heavy, black eye-makeup, and pink rouge. He was with a couple of similarly attired teen boys. I attempted to speak to him, but Jeremy didn't respond.

It seemed to me that Jeremy, who had appeared to be such a nice kid earlier, had now deliberately chosen a persona designed to make him an outcast. I later heard from some church teens who knew Jeremy that this was no simple costume, that Jeremy had in fact entered a wild and possibly demonic fringe of society. And he was known among the kids for drawing offensive, dark cartoons. I suspect that Jeremy's situation is a reaction to a deep, emotional wound, possibly related to his loss of a father.

I find myself wondering if there was anything I could have done differently during those eight weeks of mentoring that would have made a difference for Jeremy. Should I have confronted the violence I saw in his cartoons? Should I have tried to do more with him aside from the mentoring classes? I didn't intend anything wrong, but was I too wrapped up in my own life to see deeply enough into the life of this kid who was hurting inside? I don't know, but I feel bad whenever I think about him. I need some kind of purgatory to be relieved of my feelings.

Can't I just pay for those mistakes I made and be done with them? And what about actual sins I have committed, where my intentions were *not* right? Those are questions for Lent.

Today is Ash Wednesday. The season of Lent has traditionally been a time for self-examination and a fresh opening of our lives before God. But it can also reflect the gloom we may feel when our sins and shortcomings run deeply in our thoughts — when we are sharply conscious of where we fall short. There are some old hymns we sometimes sing during Lent that even reflect that outlook. One is "There Is A Fountain Filled With Blood." Verse 2 says:

The dying thief rejoiced to see that fountain in his day;
And there may, though vile as he, wash all my sins away.

Or here are the words of another Lenten hymn as the author, Isaac Watts, wrote them back in 1707.

Alas! And did my Savior bleed, and did my Sovereign die?
Would he devote that sacred head for such a worm as I.

On many days, we might object to being compared to the thief crucified next to Jesus, or to being called a worm, but sometimes, when we have done something we consider downright selfish or wrong, our sense of ourselves as a good person collapses and the words "vile" and "worm" don't sound all that farfetched.

Lent then, is an excellent idea, because it calls us back to our best character goals and our commitments to follow Jesus.

And in Lent, Psalm 139 is an excellent reading. It is a strong statement that God knows us as we really are, and the psalm concludes with a sincere prayer that God will further search our hearts, reveal to us our sinfulness, and then lead us into the everlasting way of God.

The problem is, while some of us understand that God knows us and reveals to us our sinfulness, we don't take the final step of the prayer, asking to be lead into the way everlasting. We get stuck in a sort of unending purgatory. Lent, if you will, is the Protestant purgatory, but we should not forget that we also have Easter, the birth of new life, to which Christ calls us.

13

Jesus told a story — his parable of the Pharisee and the tax collector — that illustrates two ways people can view themselves in relationship to sin. The Pharisee says, "I don't have any sin"; the tax collector says, "I am sin itself."

The Pharisee is dealt with first. His behavior is obnoxious and insufferable. The Pharisee's "prayer" is more like a litany of self-praise. He only acknowledges or "thanks" God for the fact that he is "not like other people." He cites a list of obvious sinners — "thieves, rogues, adulterers," and even includes his neighbor-in-prayer, "this tax collector." Besides stipulating what he is not, this Pharisee goes on to list what he is — one so observant of the minutiae of the law that he fasts twice a week (once was all that was required) and pays the required title on his income. The Pharisee, without any sense of his own sinfulness or unworthiness, can have no true sense of God's grace.

The tax collector makes no such claims. The occupation of tax collector was a particularly despised one for first-century Jews. The tax collector made his living by collecting the taxes imposed by the occupying forces of Rome. While this would have been enough to make him unpopular on its own, the tax collector necessarily added insult to injury. Because he received no wages from the Romans to do this work, he actually earned his living by charging more than the Romans required and pocketing the profits. In effect, the tax collector was both a usurer and a user of his people. But this particular tax collector recognizes his sinfulness and asks for mercy, and of the two, only he goes away forgiven. Jesus' story helps us to see that God views people as righteous only when they recognize their own sinfulness and repent of it.

To go back to Isaac Watts' words, we could say that only because this tax collector saw himself as a "worm," was he able to be forgiven. He saw himself in true humility, and under that circumstance, "worm" is a pretty good word. The word "humility" comes from the Latin word *humus*, which means "fertile ground." The ground is always there, taken for granted, trodden upon. But because of its position and fertility, it can receive seed, give of its substance, and yield fruit.[2] The worm, of course, is a creature of the soil, co-mingling with it. It is a humble creature.

As we humble ourselves before God and strive to see what he sees within us, to view ourselves as we really are, we receive the opportunity to grow and mature further in our faith. That's part of what Lent calls us to.

One of the things that ought to keep us humble is the example of great Christians from the past. Time and again we find in their writings comments that they had experienced a fresh awareness of their sinfulness. It was not usually that they had committed some specific sin as that they sensed the great gulf between who they were and who God is. In other words, it is not so much sinful actions that are the problem as sin itself, the inner rebellion against God.

Jesus actually spent a lot of time with "tax collectors and sinners," and some of the "respectable" people objected. They saw two kinds of people: sinners and the righteous. Jesus saw only one kind: sinners. We can say there are sinners and forgiven sinners, but because of the nature of humanity, sin is not something we leave altogether behind once we become a Christian, never to be bothered by it again.

So because of that, we might like the idea of some sort of purgatory — a place where we can finally pay for and be rid of our sins, mistakes, and shortcomings. But let's settle for Lent — a time to acknowledge our unworthiness.

But let's also remember that Lent is the lead-up to Easter, and that Jesus invites us to rise forgiven, redeemed, and made whole.

---

1. Information on Finland and the measurement aspect of purgatory from Martin E. Marty, "Speedy Retribution," *Christian Century*, February 7-14, 2001, p. 71.

2. See Anthony Bloom's thought on this in *A Guide to Prayer for Ministers and Other Servants*, p. 321.

Why I Am An Optimist

A Service And
Sermon For Passion/Palm Sunday

Stan Purdum

A Service Of Worship For
Passion/Palm Sunday

Welcome and Announcements

Prelude

Call To Worship
Leader: The conquering hero rides triumphantly into the defeated city.
People: He has come to plunder and dominate.
Leader: Justice and mercy have no place in his plans.
People: Righteousness and peace are not in his vocabulary.
Leader: Jesus, our conquering Hero, is different.
People: He enters the city on a humble animal, bringing Good News to those estranged from God.
Leader: Jesus embodies God's love, justice, mercy, righteousness, and peace.
People: Blessed is he who comes in the name of the Lord!

Hymn
"Hosanna, Loud Hosanna"

Opening Prayer
O God, recalling at this moment Jesus' ride into Jerusalem, we would join the adoring crowd and be among those who proclaim his Lordship. In this service, let our praise of Jesus be sincere and heartfelt, not simply part of a crowd dynamic, but an offering from our individual open and receptive spirits. In his name we pray. Amen.

Praise
"Surely The Presence Of The Lord Is In This Place"

Heading Toward The Cross
Matthew 21:1-11

Choir Anthem

Hymn
"Come, Let Us Use The Grace Divine"

Presenting Our Offerings
Offertory
Doxology

Scripture
Philippians 2:5-11

Choir Anthem

Morning Prayer
Holy Source of all that is good and just and righteous, we sense the mood changing. The scripture we just heard speaks not of victory parades and cheering crowds, but of slavery, emptying, obedience even to the point of carrying a cross, even to the point of being carried *on* a cross. The excitement of Palm Sunday gives way to the darkness of Gethsemane and Golgotha.

We know such dramatic shifts in our own lives, too, O God. We have seen how a single piece of personal news can trump the joy of life and push us into the depths of despair.

O God, who through Jesus has gone from Palm Sunday to Good Friday, but who has defeated death and despair in the process, be with us in all of the ups and downs of our lives.

Receive our praise, in the name of the One who suffered and died and rose again. Amen.

Sermon
Why I Am An Optimist

Hymn
"When I Survey The Wondrous Cross"

Benediction

Postlude

Why I Am An Optimist

Philippians 2:5-11

I want to say something this morning about my own relationship with Christianity, and that is that being a Christian has made me a long-range optimist. What I mean by that is that whatever agonies and hard times our world may go through, however much life may be viewed as a struggle between good and evil, in the end, *God wins*. In addition — and this is important — those who are faithful to God in this life stand with the Victor at the end. Whatever pains and losses we may experience in our lives, they never have the final word. God does.

We can call this view "long-range optimism," and we affirm today that it is a primary theme underlying all Christian theology and preaching.

But let me go a step further. For much of life, some short-range optimism is warranted as well. That which we call Christian joy means that faith in Christ adds a dimension of hope and uplift to our lives that is not obliterated even when we experience major problems or catastrophes. It is something larger than the circumstances of life.

I actually try to reflect this optimism in the way I conduct our worship services. I believe that most of the time, when we gather for worship, confidence in our God should result in a spirit of enthusiasm, of hope, and of uplift. That's why friendliness, humor, up-tempo hymns, and personal testimonies of faith are always welcome in our services. When we pray for the sick and the suffering and the grieving, we do so not in a mood of "Oh, ain't it awful," but of "Thank you, because whatever happens to us, O Lord, our lives are in your hands."

Having said all of that, however, as Christians, we still have to deal with Holy Week, the seven-day period that begins today. Holy Week starts with Palm Sunday, the day Jesus rode into Jerusalem on a donkey and was greeted with wild enthusiasm by the crowd. Although the mood of the people was upbeat and the atmosphere was like that of a parade, you and I know that there was a dark undertone to the day. Though the people didn't realize it, Jesus did, and he understood that the celebration was actually the prelude to an execution.

We also know that before the week was over, one of Jesus' closest companions would betray him, another would deny even knowing him, and the rest would run away in terror. Jesus would undergo an arrest, an illegal trial on trumped-up charges, a flogging, and a crucifixion. By the time the week ended, Jesus was lying stone-cold dead in a burial cave.

That's Holy Week, my friends, and by itself, it leaves little room for optimism of any sort.

We are holding a Good Friday service later this week, which I believe will be full of meaning and will be good for us spiritually, but don't expect to leave it with toes a-tappin' and a bounce in your step. Good Friday is really Black Friday, and the observance of it is meant to remind us that Jesus really did go to the awful depths of terror, pain, loneliness, and death in being faithful to his Father's will — so low, that at one point on the cross, he cried out, "My God, my God! Why have you forsaken me?"

We also know that the new week starts with an altogether different situation. On Easter Sunday, optimism is abundantly justified. The resurrection of Jesus is the great reversal where we regain that confidence that death loses and God wins.

But before we get there, we have to deal with Holy Week. And we should, because sooner or later, in our own lives, we have to go through dark valleys that are more like Holy Week than Easter. We could even say that the eight days starting on Palm Sunday and ending on Easter are a microcosm of life itself. We start out on the upbeat note of a new, unsoiled life, a precious baby, but as we grow, eventually we have to pass through some experiences that wound us, that pull us down, that leave us depleted. Sometimes the only thing that keeps us going is the long-range optimism that no matter how bad things get here, they do not have the last word, and that the Easter world awaits for the faithful at the end of this existence.

So in the church, while we are looking forward to Easter next Sunday, we cannot skip over Holy Week. While we usually come to church to get spiritually filled up, Holy Week has the reverse effect. Instead of filling us, the scriptures about the suffering and death of Jesus tend to deflate us. We may come to church wanting assurance of the power of God, but what we find in the Holy Week stories is that Jesus is one from whom all power is taken. He cries from the cross that God has abandoned him, and then, instead of his spirit being strengthened, it is surrendered.

In the scripture reading from Philippians today, Paul tells us to let the same mind be in us that was in Jesus when, though he was in the form of God, he emptied himself, taking the form of a slave, and became obedient to the point of death. In using these words, Paul is quoting a hymn then in use in the first-century Christian community. It shows us that this understanding of Christ emptying himself did not arise as theology lacquered onto the story of Jesus at some later date. Rather, right from early after the birth of the church, Christians sang a hymn that acknowledged that Jesus *poured out* his life for others.

In this passage from Philippians, Paul goes on to talk about the subsequent exaltation of Christ, that which we celebrate on Easter, but before he will let us get there, he first tells us that, like Jesus, we must allow ourselves to be emptied.

This makes little sense to us. For years, our mothers hounded us not to skip meals and not to burn the candle at both ends, to get enough sleep. It wasn't good for us to get down, to try to putt along on empty, they told us. And in the normal course of things, they were right.

But there are some times when we need to stop filling ourselves, and to allow our reserves and all that keeps us going to be drawn out and used up. We need to empty ourselves, not of what is worthless, but of what is the most valuable within us. That, our scripture tells us, is what Jesus did, not exploiting the best within him — his equality with God — but giving it up and allowing himself to be vulnerable to the forces arrayed against him.

Maybe that is why fasting has been part of the observance of Lent for some people. The physical emptiness of the stomach is a way to remind ourselves that to be filled by God, we need to make room for him.

Have you ever thought about why it is that the only time we hear much about missionaries is either when the church is soliciting funds to support them or when they have been kidnapped or murdered by rebel forces in the countries where they have been serving? In other words, it is only when we are reminded either how dependent they are upon the support of others or when their vulnerability makes them pawns in the hands of wicked men that our attention is drawn to them. That's because they have chosen a path that takes them out of the limelight, out of places of prestige, into places of risk and obscurity. They have emptied themselves, choosing to be obedient rather than recognized. They have followed a call downward, away from the comforts of American life, and toward humble service. They have accepted that they have to run with very little in their tanks.

Holy Week also reminds us that there are times when to love our family members or friends, we have to run on empty; we have to give the best of ourselves, even when we feel that we have nothing left to give, so that we can help them or meet their needs.

There is no doubt that running on empty is risky business. A few years ago, while I was employed in a business office, there was a woman who worked in the mailroom for a while. Like the rest of us, she participated in the 401k-pension plan our employer had arranged. Like the rest of us, too, she benefited from the contributions that our employer made to the plan to match a percentage of our personal contributions. She really liked her job there and the company was pleased with her work, but one day she resigned. Her son, a young man in his early twenties who lived in another part of the country, had gotten into some serious legal trouble, and his mother felt that she was going to need to relocate to be near him to help him out. Because she would need some money to do this, she decided to cash in her 401k plan. I recall our general manager talking to her seriously to make sure she understood the financial implications of doing that. First, because she had not been at the company enough years to be fully vested in the plan, she would lose most of the matching contributions that the company had placed in her account. Second, she would have to pay tax in the current year on the money that she withdrew, and third, she would have to pay a substantial penalty for withdrawing the money before she was at the retirement age.

She understood all of that, she said. But she needed whatever money she could get to help her son, and she saw no alternative. So she withdraw the funds, leaving herself with nothing. She emptied herself — made herself impoverished — to save her son.

And that is what Jesus did. In not running away from the agony of Holy Week, in not turning away even from the cross, he emptied himself to save the rest of us.

If we look at the crucifixion from the perspective of Easter, of course, we can see that God did not abandon Jesus at all. At the moment Jesus yielded up his life, he felt totally separated from God. He cried, "Why have you forsaken me?" But the feeling was just that, a feeling. It did not reflect reality. God was powerfully present, opening himself to the whole world through the death of his Son. In those hellish hours of desolation, God in Jesus let the impact of the world's sin, hatred, pain, loss, and grief fall upon him. Jesus' emptying himself opened the way for us to be filled with the presence of God.

So we'd best not skip Holy Week. In our moments of fear, darkness, abandonment, pain, even when, like Jesus on the cross, we feel God is far away, he is not. We can risk emptiness because we know that somehow that emptiness becomes a channel through which God can work. We can risk emptiness because Jesus did, and we know that God's fullness is the reward.

That's why I'm an optimist.

As I Have Loved You

A Maundy Thursday Service

Kirk W. Bruce

As I Have Loved You
A Maundy Thursday Service

Setting

Social Hall with tables arranged in a large square. Two smaller tables in the middle of the square arranged in a cross.

One chair set up at the top of the cross draped in a cloth to symbolize Christ's presence.

The room is darkened with light from seven candles on the cross table. One of the candles is elevated as the Christ candle.

Offering plates are on stands by the entrance. They will not be passed and the only mention is in the bulletin. The offering is designated to Hospice (or a charitable organization in your community).

On the center cross table is:

- Matzah — unleavened bread
- Wine or grape juice
- Maror (bitter herb) — endive
- Haroset — sweet honey
- Hard-boiled egg
- Salt
- Roasted lamb bone (symbol of Passover lamb; Jesus is our lamb)

Have a sample of each element near the pastor.

Two options for serving meal:

1. Have places previously set with each element of the meal.
2. Have trays with each item. One lamb bone will suffice for an entire table. A purple napkin can be set at each place. It can be meaningful if someone in the congregation bakes the unleavened bread.

Readers and pastor are seated together with the congregation at the ring of tables around the cross-shaped tables.

Parts

Pastor

Four readers (Reader #1 shares many of Jesus' own words)

Appoint someone to extinguish the candles at the appropriate times.

* * * * *

Pastor: Welcome to Maundy Thursday worship. In John's telling of the event of the Last Supper, after Jesus washed the disciples' feet and spoke of his coming betrayal and Peter's denial of him, Jesus imparts to them a new calling. "A new command I give to you: love one another as I have loved you. By this all men will know that you are my disciples, if you love one another." Maundy Thursday draws its name from this event; *Maundy* is Latin for mandate or commandment.

This evening, imagine we are gathered around the table with Christ Jesus as well. As he washes your feet he looks into your eyes and says,

(John 13:34-38)
Reader 1: A new command I give to you. Love one another as I have loved you. My children, I am only going to be with you a little while longer. You will look for me, and just as I told the Jews, so I will tell you now: Where I am going you cannot come.

Reader 2: Where are you going?

Reader 1: Where I am going, you cannot follow now, but you will follow later.

Reader 2: Why can't I follow you now? I will lay down my life for you.

Reader 1: Will you really lay down your life for me? I tell you the truth, yet before the rooster crows, you will deny that you even know me.

Pastor: It is around the Lord's table that we have gathered to-night. In this time of prelude, I invite you to meditate and feel his company and presence.

Soft Piano Prelude

Call To Worship (*edited from* UCC Book of Worship, *p. 193*)

Pastor: We are gathered in the presence of God, who asks us to choose between life and death.

All: **We are gathered like the people of Israel, who were challenged to choose the way of life.**

Pastor: Like them we often follow the ways of death.

All: **Yet like them, we have the freedom by the grace of God, to begin each day anew.**

Pastor: By our presence here this evening, we are saying that we choose life.

All: **Let us praise the God of love and life, who has called us to this place.**

Hymn
"Beneath The Cross Of Jesus"

Pastor: For the Jew every meal was a religious experience, and the Passover meal was the most important religious meal.

(*Exodus 13:3-10*)
Reader 3: Then Moses said to the people, "Commemorate this day, the day you came out of Egypt, out of the land of slavery. For seven days eat bread made without yeast and on the seventh day hold a festival to the Lord. On that day tell your son, 'I do this because of what the Lord did for me when I came out of Egypt.' This observance will be like a sign on your hand and a reminder on your forehead that the law of the Lord is to be on your lips. You must keep this ordinance at the appointed time."

(*Exodus 11:4-7*)
Pastor: And so at the first full moon after the spring equinox, the Passover is celebrated to remember how God heard the cries of Israel when they were slaves in Egypt and acted decisively in freeing them. It was the final plague, the death of the firstborn throughout all of Egypt, that changed Pharaoh's mind. About midnight God went throughout Egypt. Every firstborn son died, from the firstborn of Pharaoh to the firstborn of the slave girl, and the firstborn

31

of all the cattle as well. And there was a loud wailing throughout all of Egypt. But among the Israelites, not a dog barked at man or animal.

(*Exodus 12:1-14*)
Reader 4: Then the Lord said to Moses, "Each man is to take a lamb for his family, slaughter them at twilight, eat the meat roasted over a fire with bitter herbs, and bread made without yeast. They are to take some of the blood and put it on the sides and tops of the door frames. On that same night I will pass through Egypt and strike down the firstborn of both men and animal, the blood will be a sign and when I see the blood, I will pass over you. This is a day you are to remember, for the generations to come."

Pastor: And so the Passover was established. It was a feast that Jesus too celebrated. The annual pilgrimage to Jerusalem was a part of his faith.

(*Luke 2:41-42*)
Reader 1: Now every year his parents went to Jerusalem for the festival of the Passover. And when Jesus was twelve years old, they went up as usual for the festival.

(*Hold up the Matzah bread*)

Pastor: The bread or Matzah that is eaten is unleavened, as a re-minder that during the Exodus the Jews had to leave with such haste their dough had insufficient time to rise. Matzah therefore is a symbol of freedom. It is often circular to represent our unending need to strive for freedom.

On the first and second nights of the week-long Passover, the Seder meal is a part of the celebration. It is a festival meal much like the American Thanksgiving with a focus on the *Haggadah* or telling of the story, and several symbolic foods.

(*Hold up the lamb bone*)

Pastor: The roasted lamb bone is a reminder of the sacrificial lamb and that it was the Lord himself who redeemed the children of Israel from slavery. We are reminded by Moses that ...

(*Deuteronomy 26:8-9*)
Reader 4: The Lord brought us out of Egypt with a mighty hand and an outstretched arm, with great terror and with miraculous signs and wonders.

Pastor: It was the Lord himself

Reader 1: and not an angel

Reader 2: and not a seraph

Reader 3: and not a messenger.

Reader 4: It was the Lord and none other.

Special Music
   Choir Anthem

Reader 2: How is this night different from other nights?

Pastor: Tonight we eat unleavened bread — Matzah, bitter herbs — maror, sweet — haroset, salt, and a hard-boiled egg, and we drink wine. The bitter herbs are a reminder of the bitterness the Israelites experienced in Egypt.

(*Exodus 1:11-13*)
Reader 3: So the Egyptians put task masters over the Israelites to oppress them with forced labor, and they built store cities for Pharaoh. The more the Israelites multiplied, the more the Egyptians came to dread them and worked them ruthlessly.

Pastor: The honey into which we dip the bitter herbs symbolizes the mortar and bricks which our ancestors were forced to use in the building of cities and treasure houses for the Pharaoh.

33

(*Exodus 1:14*)
Reader 4: The Egyptians made their lives bitter with hard labor in brick and mortar.

Pastor: But life is a bittersweet experience. The sweet and pleasant taste impresses upon us that no matter how bitter the present may appear, life is sweetened by the hope we have in God. Sweet are the uses of adversity.

(*Psalm 71:10-11, 14*)
Reader 1: For my enemies speak against me; those who wait to kill me conspire together. They say God has forsaken him ... no one will rescue him ... But as for me, I will always have hope; I will praise you more and more.

All: All praise to you, O Lord our God, ruler of the universe, creator of the fruit of the earth.

Pastor: Dip with me, remembering the bitter and the sweet.

(*Dip the bitter herb into the honey; then eat*)

Pastor: The roasted egg, another holiday food, is unlike most foods. It does not become softer when it is cooked; it becomes harder. This is a reminder of the stubborn resistance of the Jewish people against those who sought to crush them. The egg, then, is also a symbol of life.

(*Psalm 126:1-3*)
Reader 3: When the Lord brought back the captives to Zion, we were like men who dreamed. Our mouths were filled with laughter, our tongues with songs of joy. Then it was said among the nations, "The Lord has done great things for them."

(*Isaiah 37:31-32*)
Reader 4: Once more a remnant of the house of Judah will take root below and bear fruit above. For out of Jerusalem will come a remnant and out of Mount Zion, a band of survivors.

Pastor: We dip our egg into the salt as a reminder of the salty tears shed by Israel in their years of oppression.

(Psalm 126:5-6)
Reader 2: Those who sow in tears will reap with songs of joy. He who goes out weeping ... will return with songs of joy.

All: All praise to you, O Lord our God, ruler of the universe, creator of the fruit of the earth.

Pastor: Dip with me, remembering the tears that were shed and new life from God.

(Dip the egg in the salt; then eat)

Pastor: It was a feast something like the one we have just had that Jesus and his followers shared. Some believe those who gathered in the upper room were more than just the disciples, and included many others who followed Jesus' teaching. Yet even while they were eating together the very forces which sought to destroy Jesus and his message were being set in motion. Jesus had just begun to walk through the darkest valley of his life. That evening would also be a test for all of his followers. Could they walk where he walked; could they drink from his cup?

The Darkness Of The Journey

(First candle is extinguished)

Hymn
"Jesus Walked This Lonesome Valley" (vv. 1, 2)

Sacrament Of Holy Communion

Pastor: Indeed it was a night very much like this one in which Jesus took those things from the table, the bread and the cup, and he blessed them. He held up the bread and said, "This is my body which is broken for you; eat this in remembrance of me." Then in the same way he took the cup and said, "This cup is my blood which is shed for you; drink this in remembrance of me."

Let us pray: Father in heaven, you revealed yourself to us in the giving of the law, the preaching of the prophets, and most fully in the gift of your son Christ Jesus who is present here with us tonight through the bread and cup. We find his body and lifeblood in our presence around the table. Bless all who partake that they may be filled with your living spirit. Amen.

(*Pass the Matzah, each person taking a piece and holding until all are ready*)

Pastor: As a symbol of our oneness in Christ we eat together. As often as you eat of this bread you participate in the body of Christ.

(*Eat the bread*)

(*Pass the tray with the cups of wine/juice on it*)

Pastor: As a symbol of our unity in Christ we drink together. Drink of it all of you, for this is the blood of the covenant which is poured out for the forgiveness of your sins.

Let us pray: O Lord, the giver of life, we ask that tonight our lives might be changed. In the receiving of Christ into our hearts and minds and lives, may we be a new creation in him, made in your holy image. Amen.

(*Drink the wine/juice*)

Pastor: Jesus was beginning the journey through the darkest night of his life. Indeed our life does have many dark times. We have all walked with Christ in the darkness of being misunderstood by our friends and our enemies. It is as if a great blanket of darkness is covering us and we want to cry out, "Don't you understand?" I wonder if his followers understood what he was doing around the table. Did anyone understand what Jesus was doing that whole week? Do we understand?

(Mark 11:15-18)
Reader 2: On reaching Jerusalem, Jesus entered the temple area and began driving out those who were buying and selling there. He overturned the tables of the money changers and the benches of those selling doves, and would not allow anyone to carry merchandise through the temple courts. And he taught them saying,

Reader 1: Is it not written, "My house will be called a house of prayer for all nations"? But you have made it a den of robbers.

Reader 3: The chief priests and the teachers of the law heard this and began looking for a way to kill him, for they feared him, because the whole crowd was amazed at his teaching.

The Darkness Of Betrayal

(Extinguish second candle)

Pastor: Has someone you trusted ever betrayed you? Jesus knew the darkness of betrayal. He knew what it was like to open up and have his trust betrayed.

(Matthew 26:20-25)
Reader 4: When evening came, Jesus was reclining at the table. And while they were eating, he said ...

Reader 1: I tell you the truth, one of you will betray me.

Reader 3: Is it I, Lord? Is it I?

Reader 2: Is it I, Lord? Is it I?

Reader 4: Is it I, Lord? Is it I?

Reader 1: One who has dipped his hand in the bowl with me will betray me.

Reader 4: Is it I, Lord? Is it I?

Reader 1: You yourself have said so.

The Darkness Of Temptation

(*Extinguish third candle*)

Pastor: At the beginning of Jesus' ministry, he was tempted by the evil one. Scriptures tell us that even though Jesus did not succumb, the evil one was not gone. He only left until a more opportune time. Now on the eve of his death, he must walk through the darkness of temptation.

(*Matthew 26:37-42*)
Reader 2: He took Peter, and the two sons of Zebedee along with him. Then he said to them ...

Reader 1: My soul is overwhelmed with sorrow to the point of death. Stay here and keep watch with me.

Reader 2: And going a little farther, he fell with his face to the ground, praying.

Reader 1: My Father, if it is possible, may this cup pass from me. (*Pauses*) Yet, not as I will, but as you will.

Reader 2: Then he returned to the disciples and found them sleeping.

Reader 1: Could you not keep watch with me for one hour? Watch and pray that you will not fall into temptation. The spirit is willing but the body is weak.

Reader 2: Jesus went away a second time and prayed.

Reader 1: Father, if it is not possible for this cup to be taken away unless I drink it, may your will be done.

The Darkness Of Injustice

(*Extinguish fourth candle*)

Pastor: We learn at an early age that human life is not always just and fair. Sometimes good things happen to bad people and bad things happen to good people. Jesus' life is an example of injustice. He was without sin, yet he bore the consequence of sin on our behalf.

(*Luke 22:66—23:4*)
Reader 4: Then the council of the elders, the chief priests, and the teachers of the law ... led Jesus off to Pilate and they began to accuse him. "We have found this man subverting our nation. He opposes paying taxes to Caesar and claims to be Christ the King." So Pilate asked Jesus, "Are you the king of the Jews?" Jesus replied ...

Reader 1: Yes, it is as you say.

Reader 4: Then Pilate announced, "I find no basis for a charge against this man." But they insisted.

The Darkness Of Rejection

(*Extinguish fifth candle*)

Pastor: In Jesus' journey through the valley of shadows Jesus also had to journey through rejection. Where were all the crowds who just a few days earlier shouted, "Hosanna"? Where were his friends with whom he had celebrated in an intimate feast only the day before?

(*Mark 15:6-14*)
Reader 2: Pilate asked, "What should I do with the one you call the king of the Jews?"

Reader 3: Crucify him, crucify him.

Reader 2: Pilate asked, "Why? What crime has he committed?" But they all shouted louder:

Reader 3: Crucify him.

The Darkness Of Denial

(*Extinguish sixth candle*)

Pastor: The darkness of denial nibbles always at our soul. There are many times that we deny our Savior. We deny Christ when we sit idly by and let injustices happen that we could have spoken up against. We deny him each time we let the opportunity slip through our fingers to stand up and voice what we believe in or fail to invite another to him. We keep company with Peter when others look at our lives and they do not see the reflection of Jesus in how we live and what we say.

(*Mark 14:66-72*)
Reader 4: While Peter was below in the courtyard, a servant girl of the high priest came by. When she saw Peter warming himself by the fire she looked at him closely and said, "You were with that Nazarene, Jesus."

Reader 3: I don't know or understand what you are talking about.

Reader 4: And again two more times he denied knowing the man Jesus. He denied knowing God's son.

Hymn
    "Were You There?" (vv. 1, 2, 3)

Pastor: We have eaten together just as Christ did with his friends. The theme of the Seder meal is remembering — remembering what God did in the past. We do remember how God acted through Moses, how God sent the prophets as teachers, and how God acted in sending Jesus. But we do more than just remember. We look for him to act in our lives today. God is a living God who is active in the present. So while we look back tonight, we also look around to see the ways in which God is acting in our world today; and we look forward to how he will be present tomorrow as well.

We have journeyed together through the darkness. But there is one candle left lit, one light that is not to be extinguished. It is the light of Christ. That light is the hope of the world.

(John 1:5)
The light shines in the darkness, and the darkness has not overcome it.

(John 8:12 and "I Am The Light Of The World," 1969, J. Strathdee)
Jesus told us he is the light of our world and he invites us to follow him. For if we follow and love, then we'll learn the mystery of all that we are meant to do and be.

As you journey through your darkness, remember you are not alone. Christ is by your side.

Benediction
Go now in silence; go in the peace of Christ and the power of Easter morning. Amen.

Postlude

(Suggestion: A prayer vigil at the church may follow the service with someone in the building praying at all times from the close of Maundy Thursday until sundown Friday.)

41

Through The Eyes Of Jesus

A Good Friday
Tenebrae Service

Douglas E. Meyer

Through The Eyes Of Jesus
A Good Friday Tenebrae Service

Introduction

A few months ago I met a middle-aged man in a nursing home who had quite a story to share with me. He's currently paralyzed from the waist down and confined to bed most of the time. He told me of how he used to be an alcoholic, was prone to getting into fights, had a failed marriage, was living apart from Christ, and, as he put it, on a one-way path to hell. But then came the day when he got down on his knees and prayed, "Whatever it takes, Lord, slow me down." Then came the accident at work that left him partially paralyzed, followed a few days later by a blood clot to the lung, which nearly took his life. As he lay there dying, he cried out to God, "Lord, please help me." And just like that, he says, the pain left, his breathing became normal, and his life changed for the better as he totally surrendered himself to Jesus. Now when I say his life changed for the better, I need to qualify that. For since then, he's been in the hospital twenty times, experienced multiple surgeries, and now resides in a nursing home. But he says he feels more peace in his life now than he ever had before.

Now what exactly does that story have to do with Good Friday? Well, while visiting this fellow one day, he told me that when he became a Christian, there was one thought, one picture, that he couldn't get out of his mind. And it was the picture of what Jesus saw from the cross when he hung there those six agonizing hours. I found that intriguing because ordinarily, especially on this day of the year, we have a tendency to look at Jesus through the eyes of the penitent thief or the Roman centurion or the mocking multitudes. But what did Jesus see as he looked down from that old rugged cross? What was his perspective? Such will be the focus of our service this evening. Let's pray:

Prayer

Father, once again we find ourselves gathered at the cross. We have come here tonight, not just to observe the humiliating and excruciating death of your Son and our Savior, but we also want to see things through his eyes in order that we might understand in perhaps a new and fresh way the magnitude and extent of all that he was willing to go through for us, just so that we could be yours for all eternity. Help us to achieve that goal, for Jesus' sake. Amen.

Choir Anthem

Scripture Reading: Luke 23:33-34

"When they came to the place called the Skull, there they crucified him, along with the criminals — one on his right, the other on his left. Jesus said, 'Father, forgive them, for they do not know what they are doing.' "

Meditation 1: The Unknowing Soldiers

The first group we want to look at this evening that Jesus saw from the vantage point of the cross consisted of his executioners — Roman soldiers whose job it was to affix him and the other two criminals to their respective crosses and then preside over this gruesome event until its desired goal had been achieved. As they went about their business, the first words from Jesus' mouth must have stunned them. For rather than cursing them, as they were no doubt most accustomed to, words of forgiveness flowed from the swollen and bloodied lips of Jesus. "Father, forgive them, for they don't know what they are doing."

But did they know what they were doing? I guess in one sense they did. They had been ordered to carry out the crucifixion of these three criminals and they were simply following orders. But in another sense, no, I'm sure they didn't know what they were doing. They didn't know that they were putting to death the only perfect man ever to live. They didn't know that they were crucifying their Creator. They didn't know that they were killing their sin-bearing Substitute. And because they didn't know that, they missed the greatest opportunity that had ever come their way — the opportunity to be delivered from the damning and eternal consequences of their sins and live in the glorious presence of God forever. Sadly, that describes many people today, many of whom we might know. So let's pray for them right now:

Prayer

Father, there are many in our world today who are like those soldiers, completely ignorant of the One who died to save them. There may even be some within our circle of acquaintances, perhaps even in our own families, who know little or nothing about Jesus. Tonight we pray for those people. We ask that you would love them through us and speak to them through us so that they might one day come to know and receive all that Jesus did for them. In his name we pray. Amen.

Hymn

"O Dearest Jesus, What Law Have You Broken?" (vv. 1, 2, 4)

Scripture Reading: Matthew 27:39-40

"Those who passed by hurled insults at him shaking their heads and saying, 'You who are going to destroy the temple and build it in three days, save yourself! Come down from the cross, if you are the Son of God!' "

Meditation 2: The Uncaring Multitudes

The second group Jesus saw from the cross was perhaps the most obvious and definitely the most numerous, namely, the uncaring multitudes. During the six hours that Jesus hung from the cross, hosts of people would have passed by — some out of curiosity, some out of a sick sense of satisfaction to see Jesus getting what they felt he deserved, but most, surprisingly, out of necessity. For remember, this was Passover week in Jerusalem and thousands of people were streaming in and out of the city on a daily basis to observe this important festival.

Many of those people were like the soldiers, completely ignorant of who Jesus was and indifferent to what was actually transpiring there that day. But then there were those who were downright cruel. The words read to you a few moments ago tell us that these people hurled insults at Jesus and scoffed at previous claims he had made. Talk about kicking a man when he's down! That's what they were doing. And that's what we sometimes do too when we skip church for the flimsiest of excuses, when we allow our

Bibles to gather dust and go unused, when we are indifferent to the spiritual needs of those around us, when we fail to give Jesus the place of honor and preeminence in our lives that he deserves. And so we pray:

Prayer
Lord, as difficult as it is, we confess to you the times that we have been like those uncaring multitudes — the times we have failed you, the times we have been indifferent to you, the times we have not honored and loved you above all things. Forgive us, Jesus. Wash us in your cleansing blood. And through the power of your Holy Spirit change us to be more like you. Amen.

Hymn
"Stricken, Smitten, And Afflicted" (vv. 1, 2, 3)

Scripture Reading: John 19:25-27
"Near the cross of Jesus stood his mother, his mother's sister, Mary the wife of Clopas, and Mary Magdalene. When Jesus saw his mother there, and the disciple whom he loved standing nearby, he said to his mother, 'Dear woman, here is your son,' and to the disciple, 'Here is your mother.' From that time on, this disciple took her into his home."

Meditation 3: His Mournful Mother
As we continue to look through the eyes of Jesus tonight, we see the one sight that must have broken his heart more than anything else. We see his mother Mary, weeping at the foot of the cross, barely able to lift her eyes and gaze upon the bloodied and disfigured countenance of her precious Son. Surely Mary's mind must have gone back about 33 years to the time when she and Joseph had brought their eight-day-old son to the temple. An old man named Simeon had appeared out of the shadows with perhaps a hint of a smile on his face. Simeon had told them that he had been promised by the Holy Spirit that he would not see death until he beheld the promised Messiah. Instantly, the Holy Spirit had revealed

to him that Jesus was that Messiah. And Simeon proclaimed his readiness to die now that that promise had been fulfilled.

But he also added something on that occasion. Turning to Mary, he spoke these mysterious words that she must have pondered over and over again: "This child is destined to cause the falling and rising of many in Israel, and to be a sign that will be spoken against, so that the thoughts of many hearts will be revealed. And a sword will pierce your own soul too." Mary felt that sword now as she finally understood what Simeon meant by those words. Let's pray:

Prayer

Father, like Mary we feel that sword tonight as we watch our Brother and our very best Friend dying, not for wrongs he had done, but for all the sins that we are guilty of. Though it isn't fair that the righteous should suffer for the unrighteous, nor the just for the unjust, we know that there was no other way for you to accomplish our redemption. And so with sword-pierced hearts we thank you for a Savior like Jesus. Amen.

Hymn

"My Jesus, I Love Thee" (vv. 1, 2)

Meditation 4: A Faithful Disciple

Along with his mother, we're told in the last passage of scripture read to you that the disciple whom Jesus loved was also present at the foot of the cross. This, of course, was John. Which automatically brings up a question: Where were the other disciples? Where was Peter who had boasted the night before that he would be willing to go to prison for Jesus and even die for him if that became necessary? Where was Thomas, who at one time had said to his fellow disciples, "Let us also go, that we may die with him," when Jesus was contemplating going to Jerusalem, knowing full well the danger that awaited him there? Where were Matthew, Philip, Bartholomew, Andrew, and the rest? Though we're not told for sure, my guess would be that they were in the same place we find them on Easter evening — in an upper room, hiding behind locked doors, scared to death that the Jews might try to do the same thing to them as they'd done to Christ.

And, oh, how it must have hurt Jesus that his closest companions in whom he had invested so much of himself did not have the courage to show up and offer him support. But, oh, how it must have warmed his heart to see the familiar tear-streaked face of John looking up at him.

May I ask you a question? Which of those two do you most resemble? The fearless disciples who failed to show up, or the beloved John who would be there for his Lord even if everyone else deserted him? Let's pray:

Prayer

Dear Jesus, you know how much we want to be like John, but how often we fail and instead end up resembling the other disciples. We are so sorry for the times we've deserted you and disappointed you, the times we've been embarrassed or ashamed to be known as one of your followers. Forgive us and give us the courage and love of John that will keep us true and faithful to you even if all others should forsake you. Amen.

Hymn

"When I Survey The Wondrous Cross" (vv. 1, 2, 4)

Scripture Reading: 1 Peter 1:18-19

"For you know that it was not with perishable things such as silver or gold that you were redeemed from the empty way of life handed down to you from your forefathers, but with the precious blood of Christ, a lamb without blemish or defect."

Meditation 5: His Own Blood

Thus far this evening we have focused upon some of the people that Jesus saw from the cross. Now we want to turn our attention to something most of you probably would not have thought of if you had just been pondering on your own what he beheld from that perspective. And that is his own blood. Blood that trickled

50

down his forehead and into his eyes from the crown of thorns. Blood that flowed from the nails that pierced his hands and feet. Blood from his scourged and shredded back that soaked the cross of wood.

When I think of that precious blood, I'm reminded of a man I visited many years ago who was a shut-in. When I brought him communion the first time in his home, he asked that I place only a tiny amount of wine in the small glass because his hands shook so much and he didn't want to spill any of it. Then he said something that I've never forgotten. He said, "One drop would save the whole world." How true! How true! For as John tells us in his first epistle, it is only the blood of Jesus, God's Son, that can cleanse us from all sins. Let's pray:

Prayer

Lord, through your servant Isaiah you told us that though our sins are as scarlet, they shall be as white as snow. Though they are red like crimson, they shall be as wool. Nothing we could ever do could accomplish that. And so we thank you that you did it all for us and that through the precious, priceless, perfect blood of Jesus our sins are completely washed away and we have peace with you. Amen.

Hymn

"Nothing But The Blood"

Scripture Reading: Matthew 27:45-46

"From the sixth hour until the ninth hour darkness came over all the land. About the ninth hour Jesus cried out in a loud voice, 'Eloi, Eloi, lama sabachthani?' — which means, 'My God, my God, why have you forsaken me?' "

Meditation 6: His Father Turns Away

Forsaken by his closest companions, rejected by the Jewish religious leaders, mocked and vilified by the uncaring multitudes, Jesus now experiences the greatest rejection of all as he beholds a sight that only he could see from the cross. He sees his own heavenly Father turning away from him and basically subjecting him to the horrors and agonies of hell.

In her book *Just Like Jesus*, Anne Graham Lotz, the daughter of Billy Graham, describes what was actually happening at this point of Jesus' Passion. She says:

> *For the first time in eternity, the Father and Son were actually separated. They were separated by all of your sins and my sins, which came between them. And Jesus, suffocating physically, was smothered spiritually by a blanket of loneliness such as he had never known.*

Why would the Father do that to his only Son? Simply because at that point Jesus was shrouded in and burdened with all the sins that had ever been committed and that ever would be committed. From the Father's perspective it was a sight that was so disgusting, so detestable, so abhorrent that he could not bear to look upon his Son. So the Father forsook him and punished him, all so that you and I would never have to know what that is like. Did we deserve that? No! That's why we call it *grace ... amazing grace!* Let's pray:

Prayer
Lord Jesus, we can't even begin to comprehend what it must have been like for you to have your own Father turn away from you. And yet we know that it was all done out of a love that is even more difficult to comprehend — a love for sinful, stubborn, unworthy, unlovable creatures like us. And so from the bottom of our hearts and the very depths of our beings, we say thank you. Thank you for such amazing grace. Amen.

Hymn
"Amazing Grace"

Scripture Reading: John 3:16-17
"For God so loved the world that he gave his one and only Son, that whoever believes in him shall not perish but have eternal

life. For God did not send his Son into the world to condemn the world, but to save the world through him."

Meditation 7: You And I

The final group that Jesus saw from the cross that day was a group of people not visible to anyone else because it was a group of people yet to be born. And the good news for us this evening is that included in that group were you and I. Did you know that you were very much on the mind of Jesus both before and after his death on the cross? That's right. The night before Jesus died, as he met with his disciples in that upper room and prayed for them, he added these words: "My prayer is not for them alone. I pray also for those who will believe in me through their message." That would include you and me for have we not believed in Jesus through the life-giving, soul-saving message of the gospel?

But there's more. You were also on Jesus' mind when he rose from the dead. When he appeared to his disciples in the upper room the week after his resurrection and this time Thomas was with them, Jesus said to the one who had doubted: "Because you have seen me, you have believed; blessed are those who have not seen and yet have believed."

Again, that's you and I, isn't it? Though we have not seen or touched the nail prints in his hands and the spear wound in his side, we still believe everything the Bible tells us about Jesus. So rest assured, you were very much on his mind and very much in his sight when he hung from the cross that dark Friday so long ago. And so we pray:

Prayer

What a comfort it is to know, Jesus, that when you were on the cross, we were on your mind. And that even though you knew in advance every sin we would ever commit, every offense that would drive those nails deeper into your hands and feet, you still loved us enough to die for us. May every person here tonight be moved by such love, inspired by such sacrifice, and changed by such grace. In your name we pray. Amen.

Solo
 "When He Was On The Cross, I Was On His Mind"

Closing Poem: Through The Eyes Of Jesus
 Through the eyes of Jesus, we see so much that day:
 The soldiers who were present and felt he had to pay
 For crimes he'd been accused of, but which he hadn't
 done.
 Yet all of that was needed so the victory might be won.

 Then there were the multitudes who scorned and scoffed
 and mocked.
 Looking at his bloody frame, they weren't even shocked.
 Instead they only laughed at him and took the time to
 jeer.
 "Why don't you come down from there and then you'll
 hear us cheer?"

 But Jesus remained there firmly anchored to the cross
 And then looked down to see and feel his greatest loss.
 Mary, his mother, looked up with tear-filled eyes.
 At this precious Son of hers who had touched so many
 lives.

 And as she felt that sword of pain pierce her grieving
 soul,
 She understood what Simeon meant so many years
 before.
 But Jesus loved his mother still, even while on the cross,
 And gave instructions to faithful John to help her
 through this loss.

 But why was John the only one who showed up there
 that day?
 Where were James and Andrew, and Peter who had so
 much to say?
 Hiding behind locked doors and fearing for their lives,
 They were frightened that the Jews would do to them
 what they'd done to Christ.

What else did Jesus see that day but his very own blood
that flowed
From nail-pierced hands and thorn-crowned scalp,
each drop of which showed
That we have a Savior whose love for us we simply
cannot measure.
So let us take that love to heart and cherish it forever.

Then came the darkest moment of all that happened
on that day.
Burdened with the sin of an evil world, his Father
turned away.
"My God, my God, you have forsaken me!" Jesus cried
alone.
Yet in that dismal cry of woe, the grace of God was
shown.

For the final group that Jesus saw as he hung on the
cross that day
Was you and me and all who'd believe that he alone is
the way.
So give to him your heart, your love, as you leave this
place tonight,
Looking through the eyes of Jesus to see a most glori-
ous sight.

That sight consists of multitudes of saints before the
throne,
Washed clean in the blood of Jesus, who will never
again be alone.
For his sacrifice on Calvary has won for you and me
A perfect home in heaven where with him we'll forever
be.

Closing Hymn
"The Old Rugged Cross" (vv. 1, 2, 4)

Behold, I Show You A Mystery

3 Choral Readings
For Easter Sunrise

Kenneth Carlson

Behold, I Show You A Mystery
An Easter Reading For Three Voices

(Voices are indicated by the numbers 1-3. Unison is number 4.)

1: Behold, I show you a mystery

2: In the beginning there was the Word

3: The Word was with God and the Word was God

4: The Word was Jesus Christ

1: The Word became flesh

2: The Word became human

3: The Word became a child born at Star's end

1: The Word became a carpenter from Nazareth

4: The Word became Jesus Christ

3: Who lived among us full of grace and truth

2: And from whom we have received grace upon grace

1: He is the Son of the Living God

2: He is the Christ of our human needs

3: He is the firstborn of the New Creation

4: He is the Word of God

1: Behold, I show you a mystery

4: And Jesus said:

2: I am the Bread of Life

3: Any who come to me shall never hunger

2: And all who believe in me shall never thirst

1: And he came to those by the sea

2: And he said:

4: Follow me

3: He came to a blind man

2: And he restored his sight

1: He came to a lame man

2: And he restored his legs

3: He came to a dead man

4: And he restored his life

1: Behold, I show you a mystery

4: And Jesus said:

2: I am the Light of the world

3: Whoever follows me shall never walk in darkness

2: But have the light of life

1: Glory be to God and to his Son, our Savior, Jesus Christ

2: In his great mercy God has given us a new birth into a living hope

3: Through the crucifixion and resurrection of Jesus, we find our hope

1: With this hope we have an inheritance that cannot perish, spoil, or fade

3: Though you have never seen him

2: You love him

3: Though you have never seen him

2: You know you are loved by him

4: For God is love

1: If you have felt this love in any small measure

2: Then you know the importance of the church

4: The Body of Christ

1: It is through the church that God brings forth his love

2: The church is God's instrument of grace

3: The church is God's covenant people

1: The church is God's fellowship of the Holy Spirit

4: The church is the Body of Christ

1: Behold, I show you a mystery

4: And Jesus said:

2: I am the Alpha and the Omega

3: I am the first and the last

1: I am the Living One

2: I was dead and behold, I am alive for ever and ever

3: Now the dwelling place of God is with humanity

2: They will be his people and he will be their God

1: And God shall wipe away every tear from their eyes

4: And death shall be no more

1: Neither mourning

2: Nor weeping

3: Neither pain

2: Nor sorrow

1: For the old order has passed away

4: And behold

2: God is making all things new

1: We are no longer children of Adam

3: But brothers and sisters of a Living Christ

1: Sin no longer has a hold on us

2: We are a part of God's New Creation in Christ

3: We may be hard pressed on every side

4: But not crushed

2: We may be confused and doubtful

4: But not driven to despair

1: We may be hurt by the adversity of life

4: But never abandoned

3: We may be struck down

4: But never destroyed

2: As Christ lives, so shall we all

1: Behold, I show you a mystery

4: And Jesus said:

2: I am the Good Shepherd

3: The Good Shepherd lays down his life for the sheep

1: Therefore, there is no condemnation for those who are in Jesus Christ

2: If God is for us

4: Who can stand against us?

1: He who did not spare his own Son

3: But gave him up for love of us

2: Will he not also give us all things with him?

1: Who shall separate us from the Love of God?

2: Shall trouble and distress?

3: Shall adversity and pain?

2: Shall doubt and confusion?

1: Shall death and denial?

4: NO!

1: For we are more than conquerors through him who loves us

2: For I am sure that neither death nor life

3: Neither powers in heaven nor powers on earth

1: Neither conflicts of today nor conflicts of tomorrow

2: Neither adversity, misfortune, or loss

3: Can separate us from the love of God in Christ Jesus, our Lord

1: Behold, I show you a mystery

4: And Jesus said:

2: I am the Way, The Truth, and the Life

3: Let not your hearts be troubled

2: Neither let them be afraid

1: Trust in God, trust also in me

2: In trusting God there is great love

3: And because of this great love for us

4: God

1: Who is rich in mercy

2: Made us alive with Christ even when we were dead in sin

3: It is by grace that we have been saved

2: And God raised us up with Christ through God's own desire and not our own

1: It is by God's grace that we are saved, and through no merit of our own

4: Salvation

3: Which is God's gift

2: Which is God's righteous desire

1: Which is God's final judgment

4: Is ours

1: And we embrace this gift through faith

2: It is God's gracious gift for we are God's beloved

3: Created in Christ Jesus to express goodness and truth

2: We are the New Creation

4: Founded on grace

1: And expressed through faith

2: Therefore, we are no longer foreigners and aliens

3: But fellow citizens with God's people

2: Members of God's household

4: How can this be?

1: Behold, I show you a mystery

4: And Jesus said:

2: I am the resurrection and the life

3: Even though you die, yet shall you live

4: This is our hope

1: In the darkness of night

4: This is our hope

2: In our struggles over sin

4: This is our hope

3: For all that is yet to come

1: Through faith in God and our redeemer Christ

4: Death is not the final word

2: We shall not sleep

3: We shall be changed

4: In a flash

1: In the twinkling of an eye

2: In a moment of glory

3: Death is swallowed up in victory

1: Where, O death, is now your victory?

2: Where, O death, is now your sting?

3: The sting of death is sin

2: The sting of death is not trusting in God

1: The darkness of death is not trusting in Christ

3: The power of sin is a faithless heart

2: The sting of death is believing that death is the final word

1: The darkness of death is believing that God does not love us

2: That God does not embrace us

3: That God does not forgive us

1: The power of sin is the faithless heart that does not believe in the mystery of Christ

2: How One so abundantly alive with the presence of God

4: Could become a part of God

3: How One so abundantly alive could be crucified, dead, and buried

2: And yet not perish in the darkness of death

1: How One so close to God could reach out with spiritual arms

2: And embrace the world that denied him

4: Betrayed him

3: Beat and wounded him

1: Behold, I show you a mystery

2: "Father, forgive them for they know not what they do"

3: God's love for us extends beyond faith to God's own desire

1: How God in Christ could take a loaf of bread

4: Bless and break it

2: And give it to the world as a symbol of his abundant life

1: How God in Christ could take the cup

4: Bless it and share it

3: And call it his blood

1: The life essence of a New Creation

4: A new relationship

2: A new expression of faith not founded on merit

3: But founded on God's love for us

4: For God so loved the world

1: The bread and cup are shared forever in remembrance of Jesus Christ

2: In remembrance of who Jesus was

4: And who we are

3: In remembrance of God's eternal promise to be with us forever

1: Behold, I show you a mystery

2: On the first day of the week very early in the morning

3: The women took the spices they had prepared

4: And went to the tomb

1: They found the stone had been rolled away

2: They found the tomb was empty

4: They were frightened

3: They thought someone had stolen the body

2: But voices were heard to say:

4: Do not be afraid

2: I know that you are looking for Jesus who was crucified

1: Dead

3: And buried

4: And he is not here

1: He is not dead

4: He is alive

2: He has gone on before you to prepare the way

3: He has gone on before you as the Light that shines in darkness

1: He has gone on before you as the Gift that conquers death

4: And Thomas said:

2: I will not believe until I have touched him

3: Blessed are those who believe but have not touched him

1: Behold, I show you a mystery

2: You may not have touched the Living Christ

3: But the Living Christ has touched you

4: He has claimed you as his own

3: Through his wounds you are healed

2: Through his grace you are forgiven

1: Through his love you are a child of God

4: Through his death you will live forever

3: I once was blind but now I see

2: I once was lost but now am found

1: Thanks be to God who gives us this victory over sin and death

4: Thanks be to God

1: Amen

2/3: Amen

4: Amen

Caterpillars And Butterflies
An Easter Reading For Three Voices

(Voices are indicated by the numbers 1-3. Unison is number 4.)

1: Once upon a time in a beautiful garden there lived a family of caterpillars

2: Some of them were small and slender

1: While others were large and round

3: Some were smooth

1: And some were fuzzy

2: But they were all caterpillars and lived together in this beautiful garden

4: They were happy with their garden

3: It had flowers and soft grass

1: And more than enough leaves for them to eat

2: The days were never too hot

3: Nor the nights too cold

1: It was a perfect, peaceful garden

4: And the caterpillars were very happy

2: They spent their days eating the soft, tender leaves of the plants that grew in the garden

3: They spent their nights curled up in tight little balls of fur

1: Or curled around each other, using each other's warmth as blankets

3: Every morning they would get up, locate the next tender bunch of leaves, and eat throughout the entire day

2: And every night they would curl up next to each other and sleep

1: Day after day

2: Night after night

4: The same old thing

3: As enjoyable as the garden was, some of the caterpillars began to wonder

1: Is this all there is to the meaning of life?

2: We eat

3: We sleep

2: We eat

3: We sleep

2: We eat

3: We sleep

1: And we eat some more

4: What's the purpose?

3: Suddenly something very strange happened

2: Having eaten so many leaves, the caterpillars had grown too large for their skins

3: One by one they started to rip apart down their backs

4: They were scared

1: No one told them this would happen

2: They thought they were dying

1: One of the caterpillars shouted out to the others:

3: "I told you we shouldn't have eaten so much"

1: Just as suddenly as they started to split their old skins

4: The experience was over

2: All around them were pieces of their old selves

3: They had grown so large from eating all day

4: They had grown new skins

1: They had not died

4: They had only grown

2: And they learned that growing was good and they shouldn't be afraid

1: Growing was natural and in some ways fun

2: Oh, there was a little pain as the old skins started to split

3: But the new skins were so much prettier than the old ones

1: They soon forgot the pain and began to enjoy the garden once more

3: Yet it was back to the old routine

1: Eat all day

2: Sleep all night

1: Eat all day

2: Sleep all night

4: It was boring

1: And they still wondered if this was all there was to life

3: Once when two caterpillars found themselves eating the same leaf, a fight started

1: One said that she had the leaf first

2: But the other said it didn't matter and kept eating

3: This was something new, they thought

4: Fighting over food

2: It broke the routine of eating and sleeping

3: But it scared the smaller caterpillars

1: If fighting became the rule for eating

3: Then the little ones would be left out

4: It didn't seem fair

2: The larger caterpillars said that fairness had nothing to do with it

4: It was all about survival

1: If the smaller ones couldn't keep up

2: Then they would just have to die

3: The larger the caterpillars grew

4: The nastier they became

3: Especially toward the little ones

1: Soon their new skins were growing long spikes from top to bottom

2: This made the fighting even worse

3: Friends would become enemies over the possession of the same leaf

2: They would try to spike each other to gain control of the food

1: Some of the caterpillars were badly hurt

3: And some of them even died

4: This didn't seem right

1: There was plenty of food to go around

2: It just seemed that the larger caterpillars enjoyed taking control of the garden and hurting the little ones

1: Even though this upset the balance of the garden

4: The routine never changed

3: Eat

1: Sleep

3: Eat

1: Sleep

3: Eat

1: Sleep

4: And shed their skins

2: Then one day something miraculous happened

4: The routine stopped

1: The caterpillars no longer felt like eating

2: And they didn't feel like sleeping

1: They just stopped where they were and tried to figure out what was happening

3: Some thought they were just going through another stage of shedding their skins

2: But others thought something quite new was happening

1: Then one by one the caterpillars started hanging from the branches

3: By a thin thread of silk they hung upside down

2: Then one by one they started to create a cocoon

1: They didn't know what was happening or why

3: It only seemed like the right thing to do

4: There they hung

1: Just swinging in the soft breezes of the garden

4: Waiting for something to happen

3: One day after an especially beautiful sunrise

2: The garden was bathed in the warmth of a glowing summer morning

1: It should have made a sound, but it didn't

2: One by one the cocoons started to crack open

4: The caterpillars were gone

3: The dangerous spikes that had grown on their backs were transformed into beautiful wings

1: Their hungry mouths equipped for chewing had now turned into elegant long tongues equipped for sucking nectar from flowers

2: Some of the new creatures had grown slender long antennae

3: While others grew fuzzy feathered ones

1: But the most remarkable feature of these transformed caterpillars was their wings

3: Some were orange with black stripes

2: Some were red with black spots

1: Others were white and yellow and even blue

3: They were a rainbow of colors waiting in the sunlight for their wings to dry so they could stretch them out and fly

2: It was a miracle of God that little fuzzy wormlike caterpillars

3: Some with nasty tempers

2: Could be transformed into beautiful multicolored butterflies and moths

3: From ground-bound caterpillars they had become beautiful creatures that could fly and swoop and visit other gardens all over the neighborhood and beyond

1: As butterflies and moths they had discovered many new reasons for living

2: They were no longer competitive for food

1: They would no longer fight and cause harm to themselves and others

3: With their ability to fly they knew there was food to feed their need

2: They would add glorious color to the neighborhood and backyards

4: They would be admired

1: And praised for their flight and beauty

3: And they knew that this too was a part of their reason for living

2: But most importantly they would help the flowers and shrubs multiply by bringing pollen from one plant to another

1: And all over the neighborhood

2: New flowers would grow year after year

4: From caterpillars to butterflies

3: From competitive ground-bound creatures

2: To cooperative and peaceful creatures of the daylight sky

4: From caterpillars fearful of growth

1: To butterflies and moths

2: The beautiful result of faithful growth

3: From the lost to the found

2: From the blind to those who see

1: God has a way of working on our behalf to restore beauty and honor to the human soul

3: And cooperation and love to the human community

4: Where there is waste

2: We will co-create with God the resources for growth and community

4: Where there is loss

1: We will co-create with God's Spirit a climate of comfort and encouragement

4: Where there is despair

3: We will co-create with Christ the faith that transforms futility into hope

2: Darkness into light

1: Indifference into love

4: For love never fails

3: We will all be transformed from the ground-crawling caterpillars of yesterday

2: Into the beautiful sky-flying butterflies of tomorrow

3: All our prayers have taken wing

1: As Christ was raised from the dead

2: So we shall be raised from the moments of darkness and despair

1: We shall all fly with wings as eagles

2: Butterflies

3: Moths

4: We shall all be transformed

1: No one shall hurt or destroy anything God has created

3: And the living presence of our loving God shall remain with us always

4: Amen! Amen!

I Will Be With You Always
An Easter Reading For Mixed Voices

(Voices are indicated by the numbers 1-4. Unison is number 5.)

5: It was quiet

1: In the predawn stillness of slumber

4: In the silence of a sleeping world

5: It was quiet

3: As the sun peeked over the horizon

2: And the night chill rose from the earth

4: The ways of nature were changing the guard

1: Creatures of the night were settling down for the daylight rest

2: While creatures of the day were rising from nighttime slumber

3: It was quiet on that morning

5: The second morning after the death of Jesus

1: It had been a painful death

3: An eventful death

2: A death filled with wonder and grief

4: It had been a forgiving death

3: It had been a terrifying death

1/2: He cried out in thirst

3/4: He cried out in pain

5: He cried out in sorrow

4: "My God, my God, why have you forsaken me?"

1: He cried out in faith

3: "Father, into your hands I commit my Spirit."

1: He cried out in triumph

2: "It is finished!"

1: He cried out his last breath

4: Closed his eyes

5: And died

3: It was a quiet morning as the women came to the tomb

2: They remembered as they walked

4: They knew it was Joseph of Arimathea who had claimed the body

3: It was Joseph and Nicodemus who brought him down from the cross

1: They were gentle so as not to break a bone

2: They were gentle for it was their Lord they carried

2/3: They were tender and gentle

4: Giving back to Jesus what they had received

3: Reminding everyone of the good news he had brought

1/2: Blessings from the mount

3/4: Gifts from the shoreline

1/3: Forgiveness from the Cross

2/4: Faithfulness from his death

1: They laid him in the tomb

5: It was Joseph's tomb

2: They laid him down with honor and grief

4: A stone was rolled across the entrance

3: Guards were placed on either side of the doorway

1: The women remembered and wondered

2: On this quiet and glorious morning they wondered

4: Who would roll away the stone

3: Who would help them anoint the body

1: Who would help them grieve their Lord

2: Who would help them release the pain of promises denied

4: Promises forsaken

3: Promises dead and buried with their Master

2: Who would help them release the pain of betrayed faith

1: Betrayed discipleship

3: Betrayed commitment

4: Who would help them forgive Judas

2: Who would help them forgive Peter

3: Who would help them forgive themselves

4: For they had all betrayed him

1: From the night he broke bread

3: And blessed the cup

1: From the night he prayed in the Garden

4: While his disciples slept

1: From the night he was arrested

2: To the day the crowds yelled

5: "Crucify him! Crucify him! Give us Barabbas!"

4: They had all betrayed their Lord

1: No one stepped forward to counter the crowd

2: No one stepped forward to claim his leadership

3: No one came to his aid but one

3/4: Simon the Cyrene

1: But even Simon did not do so with joy

2: He was grabbed by the guards

3: And ordered to carry the cross

4: You cannot carry the cross by command

1: You can only carry the cross by acceptance

4: This they remembered as they walked to the tomb

3: Yet still they wondered about the stone

1: It was quiet that morning

2: In the predawn moment before the women came

4: When the earth began to shake

3: And the tomb began to shudder

2: When the stone began to roll

1: And the guards began to faint in fear

3: It started with a low rumble

4: Then built to a roaring quake

2: As the earth split

4: And the stone rolled away from the tomb

1: Angels as light came to the entrance

2: They came to minister

3: They came to offer tender care

4: They came to announce good news of great joy

3: As they once did before when a Child was born

2: And shepherds came to the place of birth

1: As women now came to the place of death

5: And still they wondered

1: But to their unbelieving eyes

4: The stone had been rolled away

5: How had this been done

2: Who had the strength to move so large a stone

3: As they came closer they wondered

1/2: Where are the guards

4: As they came closer still

3/4: Where is the body

5: He is gone

2/3: Our Jesus is gone

1: A voice from the light embraced them

2: A voice from the light gave comfort to them

3: The One you look for is not here

1/2: He has risen

3/4: He is not dead

5: He is alive

4: The women were scared

3: They were frightened

2: They were amazed by the light

1: They were puzzled by the message

2: They had wondered who would move the stone

3: And it had been moved away

2: They had wondered who would help them

4: And the guards were gone

2: They wondered what had happened to the body

1: And Angels now told them he was not dead

2: Now they truly wondered

5: Could this be

1: Could One who died now be alive

4: Could the love of God move heaven and earth to return the Lord of Life

5: Where is he

2/3: Where is our Lord

1: He has gone on before you and will meet you on the way

4: Truer words were never spoken

3: Jesus had gone on before them

1: He had gone to prepare a place

2: He once said let not your heart be troubled

3: Neither let it be afraid

4: Now the good news of his word was being fulfilled

1: He has gone to prepare our place in the Kingdom of God

3: He has gone on before us and will meet us on the way

2: He meets us at the crossroads of our lives

4: He meets us in diversity and misfortune

3: He meets us in success and celebration

1: He meets us in the presence of new birth

5: And the presence of passing death

1: Jesus meets us wherever two or more are gathered

2: Jesus meets us in the solitude of prayer

3/4: In the loneliness of night

1/2: In the silence of the heart

1/4: In the sorrow of our days

2/3: And the sadness of our loss

5: Jesus meets us

1: For he who was dead is now alive

2: And he leads us with the cords of human kindness

4: And the ties of love

3: He makes his presence known in the worship of shared faith

1: He makes his love known in the gifts of service and compassion

4: Why do you look for the living among the dead

2: He is not here

5: He is risen

1: As he said he would

3: He is among us now

4: In the lights of candles

2: In the singing of hymns

1: In the hugs of friendship

3: And the embrace of strangers

4: In the heart strangely warmed

3: And the gift freely given

1: He is the living Son of our eternal God

2: And from his words we build our faith

5: "I am with you always

4: Even until the end of the world"

About The Authors

Stan Purdum is the pastor of Centenary United Methodist Church in Waynesburg, Ohio. He is also the editor of the CSS preaching journal *Emphasis*, and has written extensively for both the religious and secular press. Purdum is the author of *Roll Around Heaven All Day* and *Playing In Traffic*, both accounts of his long-distance bicycle journeys, as well as *New Mercies I See* (CSS), a collection of parish stories revealing God's grace.

Kirk W. Bruce is currently the pastor of Pilgrim United Church of Christ in Cuyahoga Falls, Ohio. He earned his B.A. degree in Marketing and Management from Mount Union College, his M.B.A. degree from Miami University, and his M.Div. degree from Methodist Theological School. Bruce is the author of *Into Your Hands* (CSS).

Douglas E. Meyer is a graduate of Concordia College (B.A.) and Concordia Theological Seminary (M.Div.) in Fort Wayne, Indiana. He has pastored parishes in Florida and Illinois, and currently serves at Salem Lutheran Church (LC-MS) in Salem, Illinois. He is also the author of *Two Good Friday Tenebrae Services* (CSS).

Kenneth Carlson is an ordained United Methodist elder who is currently the pastor of Rifle United Methodist-Presbyterian Church in Rifle, Colorado. He is a former radio disk jockey, as well as a song and story writer whose credits include two tapes of recorded music. Carlson is a graduate of Morningside College and Iliff School of Theology.